W9-BEJ-392

SPORTS GREAT SHAQUILLE O'NEAL

—Sports Great Books —

T 12082

SPORTS GREAT SHAQUILLE O'NEAL

Michael J. Sullivan

—Sports Great Books—

ENSLOW PUBLISHERS, INC.

44 Fadem Road   P.O. Box 38
Box 699   Aldershot
Springfield, N.J. 07081   Hants GU12 6BP
U.S.A.   U.K.

NORTHEASTERN
MIDDLE SCHOOL LIBRARY

Copyright © 1995 by Michael J. Sullivan

All rights reserved.

No part of this book may be reproduced by any means
without the written permission of the publisher.

Library of Congress Cataloging-in-Publication Data

Sullivan, Michael John, 1960-
  Sports great Shaquille O'Neal / Michael J. Sullivan
      p. cm. — (Sports great books)
  Includes index.
  ISBN 0-89490-594-5
  1. O'Neal, Shaquille—Juvenile literature. 2. Basketball players—United
States—Biography—Juvenile literature. [1. O'Neal, Shaquille. 2. Basketball players.
3. Afro-Americans—Biography.] I. Title. II. Series.
GV884.O54S94 1994
796.323'092—dc20
[B]
                                                                    94-30536
                                                                         CIP
                                                                          AC
Printed in the United States of America

10 9 8 7 6 5 4 3 2

Illustration Credits: Barry Gossage, pp. 9, 11, 13, 34, 36, 38, 53, 56, 58; Bob
Greene/Paramount Pictures, pp. 42, 43; Neil Leifer/Paramount Pictures, p. 45; Brad
Messina/LSU, pp. 16, 18, 19, 21, 24, 26, 28, 47.

Cover Illustration: Barry Gossage

Contents

Chapter 1

The Orlando Magic was off to its best start in franchise history. The team was keeping pace with the first-place New York Knicks. But was Orlando good enough to battle Patrick Ewing and New York for first place? The Magic found out on January 4, 1994.

It was a tough atmosphere. The sellout crowd of almost 19,800 fans at Madison Square Garden was hungry to see a win by the hometown Knicks. New York led Orlando by three games and many NBA experts thought the Knicks had a great chance to win the NBA championship in 1994.

Shaquille O'Neal had been in many arenas where the fans were loud so the noise at Madison Square Garden did not make him nervous. "Only twenty-eight games into his second NBA season," MSG Network announcer and NBC play-by-play man, Marv Albert, was telling a national audience on cable, "Shaquille O'Neal has made major strides."

Albert was right. For the Magic to be challenging for first place in only Shaquille's second NBA season was remarkable. The big man was leading the NBA in scoring with almost 29 points a game and was second in rebounds with 12.8 per contest. But the Knicks had a plan to stop O'Neal. Every time Shaquille got the ball, there would be at least three Knicks surrounding him. In the first quarter O'Neal was able to shoot only once and he missed. In addition, Shaquille was called for two fouls in the first six minutes. Magic coach Brian Hill had to sit O'Neal down so that he wouldn't pick up any more fouls before the second quarter. NBA rules state that if a player has six fouls, he is disqualified and cannot come back into the game. So Shaq's foul problems immediately gave the Knicks an advantage.

"Obviously, when you lose a player like Shaquille O'Neal you are going to suffer as a team," Knicks coach Pat Reilly said. "He is one of the best players in the NBA and he's a vital part of their team. He is a tremendous disruption to anybody's offense when he is in there. We were hoping we would get him into foul trouble early and we did."

O'Neal didn't sit for long—because while he was sitting on the bench the Knicks built up a 10-point lead. Coach Hill could not wait any longer. O'Neal was put back in at the beginning of the second quarter. Shaq scored his first point with 9:50 left in the second on a foul shot. The Knicks were still triple-teaming him every time he touched the ball. However, he didn't let it bother him. Shaquille could still help out the Magic in other ways. He blocked a shot by Knicks center Herb Williams, and the result was a basket by the Magic's Anfernee Hardaway.

The Magic slowly started to move closer to the Knicks. O'Neal finally had a chance to show the New York fans why many NBA sportswriters thought that he was the early favorite for Most Valuable Player. Shaquille stole the ball from New York center Patrick Ewing. The ball went to Magic point guard Scott Skiles, who passed it to his teammate

Shaquille goes over a defender for two points.

Dennis Scott along the right side. Instead of watching the action downcourt like most centers in the NBA do, Shaquille ran down the court as fast as he could. Scott spotted his big man running down the middle and gave him a pass. O'Neal caught the ball in stride and in one motion slammed the ball through the basket. "Woooo," roared the Knicks fans. They had finally seen what everybody in the NBA was talking about. The slam dunk by Shaquille had moved the Magic to within 1 point.

Orlando did manage to squeeze out a 1-point lead at 36–35 with 4:27 left in the second quarter, but O'Neal was called for his third foul one minute later. Again, he had to sit down. While Shaquille was on the court, the Magic had erased a 10-point lead. But with him on the bench, Orlando trailed by 6 points going into the third quarter. "The presence of Shaquille O'Neal is causing problems for the Knicks," said MSG commentator John Andreise. "That big hand of his is an imposing threat. Always threatening the Knicks with a block."

Shaq had played only 14 minutes in the first half and scored just 4 points because of his foul problems. But he was ready to start the third quarter. However, the Knicks continued to put three players on Shaquille. It was up to O'Neal's teammates to hit the open shots they got.

The Knicks started to pull away and at one point in the third they led by 11 points. Shaq didn't panic. He got the ball down low and again was surrounded by three Knicks. Instead of trying to take an impossible shot he saw Scott open by the 3-point line and he passed the ball to him. A 3-pointer for Scott! Now the Knicks were worried. If the other Magic players started hitting their open shots, the Knicks would not be able to triple-team Shaquille.

Shaq attacked. First, he faked Ewing into the air, drove

Shaq looks for an open teammate. Some opponents triple-team Shaq to stop him from making one of his famous slam dunks.

around him, and scored over Charles Oakley. On the next possession, the ball again came down low to O'Neal, who spun to his right and hit a beautiful spinning jumper. Two possessions later, the Magic stole the ball. Skiles saw Shaquille running down the middle. He threw the pass to Shaq, who dunked! The next time the Magic had the ball Skiles again threw a pass to O'Neal near the basket. Shaq turned to face Ewing. He took a fade-away jumper. Good! The Knicks called time-out! The Magic now trailed by 6 points entering the fourth quarter.

The crowd at Madison Square Garden was nervous. Earlier in the third quarter, it had looked as if the Knicks were going to blow out the Magic, but Shaquille led his team back into the game—and he did not stop. He out-rebounded both Oakley and Ewing on a missed Skiles jump shot and took one step toward the basket. Waiting for him was Knicks forward Anthony Bonner. Poor Anthony. He thought he could block Shaquille's shot. Slammmm! Foul on Bonner! It was now a Knicks 1-point lead with less than eight minutes to go.

Knicks guard John Starks raced down the court but O'Neal was waiting for him. Shaq deflected his shot to Skiles, who passed to Hardaway. Dunk! The Magic now led! The Knicks called time-out again.

The Magic got the ball back and immediately Shaquille slammed home another basket for Orlando's 3-point lead. But the Knicks were not going to give up. Starks kept on hitting jumpers. He didn't dare to try and go inside again on Shaquille. But O'Neal continued to score. His dunk and foul shot gave the Magic the lead again at 85–83. Then 6 straight Knicks points gave New York an 89–85 advantage. The fans were roaring again. They sat down quickly after O'Neal spun left and turned back to his right. He hit a shot from the right

Under pressure from Felton Spencer of the Utah Jazz, Shaq makes a layup.

baseline and then fed Scott for a 3-pointer to move Orlando ahead 90–89 with 2:56 left.

After Starks hit another jumper to put New York ahead by a point, O'Neal showed he could do more than dunk and block shots. He received a pass by the left side of the basket. Instead of moving toward the baseline, he spun toward the middle and tossed up a soft right-handed hook shot. The shot rose just above Ewing's left hand and fell softly through the basket. The Magic led again, 92–91, with 2:10 left. Ten seconds later, O'Neal was called for his fifth foul. One more foul and Shaquille would not be allowed to play anymore.

Ewing made one foul shot to tie the score. Then, in the last two minutes, something went wrong for the Magic: They forgot about Shaquille. Even though Shaquille was being triple-teamed at times, it was Scott who took the shots in the closing moments. Scott could not hit three 3-point shots. The Knicks seized the advantage and edged the Magic in a hard-fought exciting battle, 100–95.

The Magic learned a hard lesson that night. They had to get the ball to Shaquille when they were in trouble. If Shaq was being triple-teamed, his teammates had to hit their open jumpers.

But the Orlando team proved that they were ready to challenge the Knicks for the NBA title. Most Magic fans and NBA experts had thought that O'Neal's presence would eventually move Orlando closer to an NBA championship—but not this soon. It was hard to believe that all of this was happening in Shaquille's second NBA season.

Chapter 2

Shaquille O'Neal was born on March 6, 1972, in Newark, New Jersey. Despite his above-normal size and weight now, the newborn Shaq weighed in at just seven pounds, eleven ounces.

"My mother wanted me to have a first name that was unique," Shaquille later said, "and one day when she was looking through a book of Islamic names, she came upon it. Shaquille Rashuan, which means 'Little Warrior.' I was never little, but I was always a warrior."

The warrior in Shaquille kept his mother, Lucille O'Neal, his grandmother, Odessa, and his stepfather, Philip Harrison, very busy. (Shaq's biological father had left him and his mother shortly after he was born.) O'Neal was like many children—he was curious and wanted to explore the world. Even as a baby, O'Neal had a wonderful appetite. "I was a sneaky kid," Shaq said. "My mother and grandmother used to hide extra bottles (with milk) in my room. I was the kind of kid that used to hunt them down and drink them all!"

Shaquille's father, who always believed in discipline,

wanted his family to have a better standard of living than he had had when he was growing up. So Harrison joined the U.S. Army when Shaquille was just two years old.

Having their father in the Army wasn't very easy for Shaquille and his family. It meant they had to move around quite a bit. When Shaquille was halfway through the first grade, Philip Harrison was transferred to Bayonne, New Jersey. O'Neal's family now lived on an Army base. It would be that way until Shaq entered Louisiana State University some eleven years later.

Shaq did not have much time to make friends. When he was in the third grade, his father was transferred again. This time the family was moved to Eatontown, New Jersey, about fifteen minutes from the Jersey shore. Before Shaquille had a chance to get to know his new friends, his father was told, he

At the playground, Shaq relaxes with some of his young friends. When he was young, he sometimes had trouble making friends because his family moved often.

would have to move again. Now Shaq's new residence was down South—at Fort Stewart, Georgia.

By the time Shaquille was ten, it was becoming awfully hard for him to make friends. Because he was bigger than most of the other kids in school, people thought that Shaq was mean. They also made fun of his unusual name. O'Neal often ended up in fights at school. Then, when he got home, his mother and father would punish him for his misbehavior.

By the time O'Neal was a teenager, though, he stopped fighting and took up dancing. "I was really good at it," Shaquille said. "I was never clumsy. I was never handicapped by my size. I think my parents were secretly proud of me. I probably inherited the ability from my mother, who is a very graceful woman."

Shaq used to do all types of dancing, including break dancing. He was finally starting to make some friends when, yet again, he had to move. This time, his father was transferred out of the United States. Shaq said good-bye to all his sixth-grade friends and went with his family to Germany. It was a rough situation for Shaquille, who didn't know anybody there. But he still made his parents proud of him.

"I will say with some pride that I never got into drugs and alcohol," O'Neal said. "There were kids doing drugs, even on the Army base, but that wasn't for me. I was always scared of dying from some kind of overdose—same thing with booze. I took a sip of beer once and the only word I can find for it is 'nasty.' I don't like the taste of it and I don't like what it does to you."

His father's guidance molded Shaq into the kind, hardworking person he is today. "His father did a terrific job in keeping him in line," said Herb More, who was one of Shaquille's high school coaches. "Not only did his father do a terrific job but his mother was also a major factor. I think

Shaquille ended up with his mother's personality. Shaquille, when I first met him, was one of the most incredible kids. He had such a warm personality and a great smile. He would light a room with his smile. He also has a terrific sense of humor. He should be proud and his parents should be proud of him. He turned out to be one terrific person."

Shaq did have his difficulties in Germany, though. By the time he was fourteen years old, he was six feet seven inches tall. Shaq suffered from Osgood-Schlatter disease, a disease that affects the bones of young people, especially boys. Shaq had it in his knees, which were very painful. He had to rest, and drink plenty of milk to provide the calcium his bones needed to combat the disease. Slowly, the pain began to go away.

Shaq takes time-out from a game at Louisiana State University. As a teenager, he had a bone disease in his knees that forced him to rest and take time away from basketball.

The monster slam that brought Shaq attention in college was first perfected in high school.

Shaq's biggest break in Germany was meeting Louisiana State University's head basketball coach, Dale Brown. Coach Brown was teaching a clinic for youngsters. The two instantly hit it off. They kept in touch after the clinic ended. O'Neal asked Brown for some advice on how to increase his leg and upper-body strength. Brown recommended a Nautilus program and gave Shaq some literature to help him overcome his leg and upper-body weakness. Because of Shaq's size, Brown thought he was talking to a soldier! "I'm not in the Army," Shaq told him. "I'm only thirteen." But what amazed Brown even more was that Shaq wasn't on his high school's basketball team.

In O'Neal's second year of high school in Germany, his dad was transferred back to the United States. The family was now living on an Army base in San Antonio, Texas. Shaq tried out his basketball skills for Cole High School. "When he walked in to our practice I thought, 'Wow, this is some opportunity,'" Herb More recalled. "He was just great from day one. He was respectful. He was hardworking. He always listened to you. And he gave us input, too. He picked up the game real fast."

O'Neal started to impress people with his basketball skills. He began to gain weight and to improve his physical strength in his legs and upper body. He was now able to dunk without much difficulty. Shaq was beginning to perfect his monster slams.

"I remember in one particular game we were playing a rival school down here," More said. "The coach came over and said his team was going to beat us. We kind of laughed by the bench. Shaq was taking his warm-ups. But the real competitiveness came through with Shaq at that point. After Shaq finished his warm-ups, I told him what the coach said.

Shaq discusses strategy with a Louisiana State coach. Even though he was recruited by every major university, Louisiana State was always his top choice.

He just looked at me. Never said a word. But I got the message."

The ball was thrown down low to Shaquille, who spun toward the right baseline and slammed the ball through the basket. The force of the slam shook the basket and bent the rim. Play continued. Again the ball went down low to O'Neal, who faked right and dribbled left, then slammed the ball through the basket. The rim was bent again. "The third time Shaquille did the same thing and the other coach was complaining," More said. "But Shaq wasn't hanging on the rim. He was so intense that the force of his dunks bent the rim. They had to play on that bent rim the second half."

At the start of his senior year at Cole High School, Shaquille was one of the biggest names being recruited. Every college and university wanted to have him attend their school. But O'Neal still remembered the help that LSU coach Dale Brown had given him. So he ended the recruiting speculation early in his senior year by choosing LSU over schools like Kentucky, UCLA, North Carolina, Duke, Indiana, Michigan, and Ohio State.

"We were quite fortunate to get a player and a person like Shaquille O'Neal to come to our school," said Brown. "He had a terrific attitude. He always listened to you. He wanted to become the best basketball player he could. He gave us so many great memories here at LSU. It was great to have him here for three years."

At LSU, Shaq piled up the points and rebounds. In 1989–90, his first year there, he averaged 14 points a game and 12 rebounds. He also blocked 115 shots and shot a sparkling 57 percent from the floor. Shaquille was just getting ready to explode onto the college basketball scene.

Chapter 3

Shaquille O'Neal's sophomore season at LSU was to be his best. He had gained confidence after his freshman year and was in tremendous shape for the start of his second. "He was college basketball's best player when he was a sophomore," LSU coach Dale Brown said. "He did everything for us that year. If people didn't know how great he was after his freshman year, they certainly knew after his sophomore season."

O'Neal finished his sophomore year as college basketball's leading rebounder with 14.7 per game. He also shot 63 percent from the floor and scored almost 28 points a game. Shaq was chosen Player of the Year by United Press International, the Associated Press, *Sports Illustrated*, and L.A. Gear. He also won the prestigious Tanqueray World Amateur Athlete of the Year Award.

Shaq set an LSU home record for scoring with 53 points against Arkansas State on December 20, 1990. He also had 25 double-point, double-rebound games—another LSU record. Shaquille had a triple-double against Florida in 1991. He

Up for the jump shot, Shaq shoots for three points. At Louisiana State, he was one of college basketball's top shooters and rebounders.

scored 31 points, pulled down 21 rebounds, and blocked 10 shots!

Because of O'Neal's terrific sophomore season, there were many basketball onlookers who thought that Shaq should leave LSU early and play in the NBA. Many also thought he shouldn't risk an injury in college. The wise move would be for O'Neal to apply for the NBA draft. He would certainly be among the top three picks.

"I think he wanted to stay in college because of the education he was receiving," Shaq's high school coach Herb More said. "His mother and father stressed that education is very important. And they wanted to see him get that degree. But Shaq, being so big, is an easy target for an opponent. He was finding out that they were pushing him more, shoving him more, and being more physical with him. I think now, looking back, he would probably have considered leaving after his sophomore year."

But Shaq stayed at LSU for his third year. Opponents were becoming rougher with him, though, and Shaq wasn't happy about it. Neither was his dad. "When you are the star, that's what happens," More explained. "Shaq has been getting pushed and shoved all of his basketball career. It was just getting a little too much during his last year at LSU."

Despite the pushing and shoving, Shaq had another great year at LSU. He scored 24 points a game and was second in the nation in rebounding with 14. He had his best season in blocks with 157 in 30 games in 1991–92. But Shaq was tired of the dangerous physical play in college. There was no doubt that he was going to be a star in the NBA. So why wait? "He made the right move leaving LSU to go to the NBA at that point," More said. "When you have a tremendous career ahead of you, why risk it by playing one more year in college?"

Shaq moves past his defender. Standing seven feet tall, Shaq was an easy target for aggressive opponents.

Shaq was ready for the NBA. Orlando had won the right to pick first in the NBA draft, held in Portland, Oregon, on June 24, 1992. There would be no question who Orlando would pick. It took just two minutes from the start of the NBA draft to answer the question. "The Orlando Magic select Shaquille O'Neal of LSU," said NBA commissioner David Stern.

There was joy and celebration in Orlando, where 10,000 people had gathered for the announcement at the Magic's arena. The Magic were going to be a real threat in the NBA because of Shaq's talent and physical presence. O'Neal had now grown to seven feet one inch and 295 pounds. He signed a seven-year contract worth $41 million. Despite the large sum of money, O'Neal was humble about his good fortune.

"I'm not about money," he said. "I'm not about seeing how many cars I can buy, or how many closets I can fill up with clothes. I make more money in one year than my father made in his entire life. But that doesn't make me a better person than him."

In Shaq's first NBA game, an exhibition contest against the Miami Heat, he showed the fans why he was the league's No. 1 pick. Shaq finished with 25 points, 6 rebounds and 3 blocked shots. He was in fine form to begin his NBA career.

O'Neal's first regular-season game was on November 6, 1992. It was also against the Miami Heat but this time in Orlando. Shaq's superstitions started to form then. He remembered that once, before a game in college, he had eaten a slice of pizza and some pasta. That night, he had played really well—so he decided to continue the tradition when he made his NBA debut. It worked wonders for both the Magic and O'Neal. He scored 12 points, pulled down 18 rebounds, and blocked 3 shots to help Orlando win, 110–100.

It was Shaquille's first desire to help the Magic improve

After three seasons at Louisiana State, Shaq made the decision to turn professional. He was the top choice of the 1992 NBA draft.

their game over the previous season. In 1991–92, Orlando had won only twenty-one games. O'Neal wanted to play for a winning team. His presence was certainly going to add more wins for the Magic. And indeed it did. Orlando finished Shaq's first month in the NBA with victories over Indiana and Charlotte. The Magic was 8–3 after only one month with Shaquille!

The next month was a rough one for the Magic. They lost six straight games before finally defeating Philadelphia at home. Shaquille had 20 points and 15 rebounds. He continued to excite the fans around the NBA with his slams and jams. Shaq's next game was against the Sacramento Kings. O'Neal was at his finest. He scored 22 points, pulled down 20 rebounds, and blocked 7 shots. He continued his assault on the Magic's NBA opponents with 28 points, 19 rebounds, and 5 blocks in a win against Utah on December 22, 1992.

O'Neal was getting better each month. He had to improve because he was playing against some of the best players in the world. "I knew I was a better player in January than I had been in November," Shaq said.

Knicks center Patrick Ewing, considered one of the NBA's best players, was in town on January 8, 1993, to face the Magic and Shaq. The Knicks and Ewing looked sharp in the first three quarters and were leading 79–67. Ewing had scored 17 points while holding O'Neal to just 11 points. However, the Magic was now a tough team to beat at home because of Shaquille. He scored 11 points in the fourth quarter and blocked Ewing's shot three times in the last twelve minutes to help the Magic win an exciting 95–94 contest. Ewing had a chance to win the game in the last second. But guess who blocked his shot? Shaq!

The Magic met the challenge of the NBA World Champion Chicago Bulls and Michael Jordan in Orlando on January 12, 1993. Shaquille was the big reason for Orlando's win over Chicago. He scored 29 points and pulled down 24 rebounds!

The Magic stayed around the .500 mark for most of January and finished the month at 18-19. Their record was a remarkable improvement over the previous season, when Orlando had won only 21 games. But Shaquille still was not happy. He would not settle for an average record. In the next game he scored 46 points against the Detroit Pistons, but Orlando still lost. This was becoming a problem for the Magic in Shaq's first season. He would score 25 to 35 points a game but would receive little offensive support. The Magic needed an outside scorer to complement Shaq's inside firepower.

Shaquille's first-half performance in 1992–93 was noticed by the fans around the NBA. He received 826,767 votes in the All-Star Game balloting, and outpolled Patrick Ewing for the starting center slot. O'Neal didn't let his supporters down. He tallied 13 points in fourteen minutes of the first two quarters. However, Shaq only played eleven more minutes in that game. The Eastern Conference team was coached by New York coach Pat Reilly, who played his center, Ewing, for most of the second half.

Shaquille didn't complain. He wanted to be ready for the second half of the season. The Magic were still playing well, finishing the month of February with a 26–25 record. Orlando had visions of making the play-offs for the first time and Shaq was the force behind that dream. The Magic team was steady throughout March, hanging close to the Indiana Pacers for the eighth and final play-off spot in the Eastern Conference. April was going to be the key month for Orlando. They had to win most of their games to qualify for the NBA play-offs. On April 13th, the Magic bashed the Milwaukee Bucks, 110–91, to keep their play-off hopes alive. But the Philadelphia 76ers defeated Orlando in the following game, 101–85. From there, it got worse. The Magic then lost to the Cleveland Cavaliers, 113–110.

Time was running out for the Magic. Shaq and his team were desperate and they played that way in their 88–79 victory over the Boston Celtics. But they were still two games out of play-off contention. Shaq continued to provide Orlando with scoring and rebounding. He had 20 points and 26 rebounds against the Washington Bullets on April 20th. The Magic moved to within one game of the Pacers. Then they had to play the Celtics again. This time the Celtics got their revenge on Shaq and the Magic. They crushed Orlando, 126–98.

The Magic needed to win their last two games and hoped that Indiana would lose twice. The Magic defeated the New Jersey Nets and the Atlanta Hawks to close out the year. Shaq scored 31 points and 18 rebounds to help provide the win over the Hawks. Orlando finished at 41–41, a twenty-game improvement over the last year, achieved with the addition of Shaquille.

Unfortunately for the Magic, Indiana also finished at 41–41. It was the fourth tiebreaker—Indiana had scored 5 more points in head-to-head confrontations with the Magic—that allowed the Pacers to go to the NBA play-offs rather than Orlando.

Shaq's first NBA season had ended. But more than basketball was waiting for the NBA's now most recognized player and personality.

Chapter 4

Shaquille O'Neal stepped onto the floor of the Great Western Arena in Phoenix, Arizona. The sellout crowd was silent for a moment, as if someone had said "Shh!" to the 17,000 Suns fans. They hadn't forgotten that in last year's contest at Phoenix the "Shaq Attack" had collapsed a basket after dunking. Then, as a matter of respect to opposing players, the crowd booed O'Neal as he made his appearance.

Shaq could not be concerned with the boos. This was an important game for the second-place Orlando Magic. They wanted to move closer to the first-place New York Knicks in the Atlantic Division of the NBA. The Magic needed Shaq. And on this night of December 19, 1993, he did not disappoint his team.

Suns' superstar Charles Barkley was just a little bit too confident playing before the home crowd. He drove past his man along the left baseline and went up toward the basket. There Barkley was greeted by Shaq, who swatted the ball away like a tennis player hitting a serve. But defense was only a small part of O'Neal's game. He drove past Phoenix center

O'Neal created the "Shaq Attack" when he collapsed a rim after a slam dunk at the Great Western Arena in Phoenix, Arizona.

Mark West and went up toward the basket. He missed his shot but picked up the rebound. Barkley stood right in front of O'Neal, ready to block it. Shaq faked his shot and Barkley jumped. With his long, powerful arms O'Neal extended the ball toward the basket. Dunk! "Oooh!" the crowd roared.

Shaq continued his dunking exhibition to the gathering excitement of the fans. Once again he dunked over West. Then he started picking on the Suns' backup center, Oliver Miller. O'Neal faked moving to his right and then spun toward his left. In one swift motion, he stretched out his right arm, basketball in hand, and slammed it through the basket! The dunk enabled the Magic to tie the Suns, 46–46, with 3:41 left in the first half.

Shaq continued his assault on the basket in the second half with several rim-rocking slams. In the last twenty-four minutes, 36 points and 15 rebounds helped the Magic to a win over a team tough to beat on their home ground. Until Shaq and Orlando snapped that streak, the Suns had won nine games in a row at home.

It was a big win for the Magic. Orlando was in the middle of a tough five-game West Coast road trip. Magic coach Brian Hill saw the trip as a test to see if Shaq and his teammates were good enough to play for the NBA championship. "We need to continue to play well and play together and we'll become a play-off team," Hill said. "Of course, we are certainly going to need Shaq every game."

Next, the Magic went to Sacramento to play the Kings. The Sacramento team had some injuries to its players, including center Duane Causwell. Shaq was ready to take advantage.

But it wasn't until the third quarter that he started to play well. He scored 12 of his 27 points in that third quarter, including three thunderous dunks over Kings center Wayman

Shaq warms up before a game. O'Neal has inspired his teammates to always play their best.

Tisdale. Shaq hit six of seven shots that pushed the Orlando lead to 17 points. The Magic beat the Kings, 97–91, to finish their West Coast road trip with three wins in five games.

O'Neal and Hill were disappointed that the Magic had lost 14 points from their 17-point lead during one stretch of the fourth quarter. "I just missed some shots," O'Neal said. "If I had made those shots it would have made a world of difference." Added Hill: "We told them at halftime, you cannot relax against this team. The Kings will make a run at you."

This was an important change of attitude for the Magic since the 1992–93 season. The Orlando players were no longer happy with just staying close to an opponent. Shaquille O'Neal was never satisfied with scoring 30 points and pulling down 15′ rebounds if his team lost. Shaq wanted to play well—but he also wanted his Orlando team to win while he was playing well.

Shaq proved he is more than a scorer. O'Neal also pulled down a game-high 17 rebounds against the Kings and had 5 assists. He also played 45 minutes—more than any of his teammates.

"Shaq is so important to the Orlando Magic," said Peter Vecsey, who is NBC's expert on the NBA. "He creates a lot of problems for other teams defensively with his offense and he's a force on defense. You have to earn your points when you go against Shaq."

The Magic finished their road trip 3-2 which also included a win over Portland. "Anytime you come out to the West Coast and return 3-2, you've done a pretty good job," Magic coach Brian Hill said. "We need to continue to play well and play together and we'll become a play-off team."

There have been times when Shaq was a terror on the offensive end but still the Magic lost. For example, back on

The Boston Celtics are one of the Magic's toughest opponents.

November 19, 1993, Shaq brought his offensive firepower to the famed Boston Garden. O'Neal was tremendous. He scored 41 points and had 10 rebounds. But the Magic lost to the Celtics, 115–106. In that game, Shaq received some support from Anfernee Hardaway (20 points) and Dennis Scott (16 points) but it was not enough. "That's the one thing that the Magic have done to improve themselves over the past year," Vecsey said. "They have surrounded Shaq with better players. They still can improve themselves and as they do, they will be a little bit closer to playing for the NBA championship."

The Magic appear to be on the right track. With O'Neal's inside offensive scoring and his excellent defensive skills, Orlando has the strength at the center position to compete for an NBA championship.

Chapter 5

Michael Jordan stunned the basketball world when he announced his retirement after leading the Chicago Bulls to their third straight NBA championship in 1993. Jordan's decision to leave the NBA caused concern among many basketball fans. Who would step up and replace Jordan as the NBA's best player? Was there anyone in the NBA who would excite the fans as much as Jordan had?

Many basketball onlookers believe Shaquille O'Neal is the player who can sell out every ticket the way Michael did while he was in the NBA. "He is one player who can sell out a building like Michael did," NBA sports commentator Peter Vecsey said. "You really don't replace a player like a Michael Jordan. But Shaquille certainly has the personality and skill to provide fans with excitement."

Since O'Neal emerged as one of the NBA's best players after his first season, the television networks have been consistently showing the Magic's key games. Today, Shaquille O'Neal is one of the most recognizable names in sports. He's young, has a great smile, and loves children. He also wants to succeed in other areas besides basketball.

One area is the field of acting. O'Neal co-starred with Nick Nolte in a basketball movie called *Blue Chips*, developed by Paramount Communications. In it, Shaquille plays a talented basketball star from New Orleans named Neon Bodeaux. Nolte is Pete Bell, head coach of the Western University Dolphins. The Dolphins are former national champions who have slipped out of the national rankings in recent years. Under pressure, Bell and the school's athletic director begin a search for players who can help to make their program a winner again. Shaquille's character is one of the players that Bell recruits.

The movie deals with money and gifts given to star athletes. Coach Bell is under pressure to win. He must make a

Shaq with his *Blue Chips* co-stars, from left to right: Nick Nolte, Matt Nover, and Anfernee Hardaway. In the movie, Shaq plays college star Neon Bodeaux.

Like his character in *Blue Chips*, Shaq is hardworking and never expects favors from anyone.

choice between winning the right way or taking a chance and breaking the rules. The movie opened across the country on February 18, 1994. It was very popular and fans enjoyed seeing Shaq put his basketball skills on the big screen. He had natural acting ability and a wonderful presence on the screen. "Billy (director William Friedkin) felt very strongly about the idea of using real basketball players," said Michele Rappaport, one of the movie's producers. "Frankly, I didn't know if we could have found good enough actors in the sports world—and Shaquille's smile just lights up the screen."

"You want a guy who has the experience that Shaquille brings to a role like this," director Friedkin said. "What you look for in an actor is intelligence and perception. He was able to do it in a way that no actor with forty years of acting experience could have done."

The movie not only showed Shaquille's acting talent but also his competitiveness. It happens everywhere Shaq goes. Even in a movie the games become intense. "The competition in this movie had to be at a very high level," said Ron Shelton, the writer of the film. "We couldn't settle for average athletes."

While the people working in the movie praised Shaq for his efforts, he himself humbly downplayed his role in the film. "I'm basically playing me," Shaq said. "Neon [his character] is the kind of guy who works hard and doesn't want favors. That's the way I am in life. I just have a different name in the movie."

True, Shaquille has never looked for favors from anyone. But he certainly puts his good fortune to work to help others. He's very concerned about people who aren't as well off as he is. Every Thanksgiving O'Neal hires a catering service to help feed the homeless in Orlando. Shaquille goes over to the hall himself to help out. Some 300 people showed up for the first

Shaq was able to show off his basketball talents in *Blue Chips*.

"Shaqsgiving" in 1992. "A lot of people had no idea who I was," Shaq said. "They thought I was just some big black brother carving turkey and spooning up rice and peas. That was cool. It didn't make a difference to me one way or the other. I've almost been where these people were. My father worked too hard for us to be homeless, but there were times when we lived in the projects in Newark when we were on food stamps."

Shaq's giving of himself is becoming a habit. He continued his kindness at Christmas in 1992. O'Neal donated several toys and cards to the Salvation Army. In addition, he bought $4,000 dollars worth of toys from Toys "R" Us to donate to kids from needy families. Shaq and his friends personally gift wrapped the presents for the youngsters. Shaq took the toys himself and dressed up as Santa Claus. The kids loved Shaquille and he loved giving them the toys. "As long as people around me are happy, I'm happy," Shaq said. "What I get involved in is what I see in my own eyes."

That was Shaq just being Shaq. O'Neal is fond of kids and constantly takes time out of his busy schedule to sign autographs or to speak to a young boy or girl. Shaquille probably got some of his generosity from his dad. In an Orlando newspaper in 1992, there was a story about a mother and her son who met a man at the Magic team store. The youngster was admiring a poster of Shaquille. The man then went to the counter and arranged to have the poster given to the youngster free. That man was Shaquille's father, Philip Harrison.

Shaquille never forgets his father. His dad may have been hard on him while he was growing up but he knows it was for the best. O'Neal is constantly reminding reporters and interviewers about how important his father's influence was on him. Shaq has always been thankful for the guidance and

Shaq poses with some of his fans. He makes several trips to high schools every year to urge kids to get an education.

NORTHEASTERN
MIDDLE SCHOOL LIBRARY

love he received from his father. He didn't want to forget thanking his father for his help. "I now had the money to go out and really thank the people who had done the most for me," Shaq told a reporter. "One day I drove a black Mercedes up to my dad's house and left the keys for him. To be able to do stuff like that for the ones you love is the best thing about having money."

Shaquille has always realized that simply having a lot of money doesn't make you a better person. He is always looking to help someone in need. Shaquille receives a lot of fan letters—so many that it is impossible for him to answer all of them. But he does try to respond to as many as possible. Although he cannot help every person in need, Shaq supports several charity organizations. At an NBA All-Star dinner in 1993, Shaquille's jersey was sold for $55,000, which went to various charities. Michael Jordan's jersey was sold for $25,000.

Shaq also tells kids to stay in high school. He makes six appearances a year alone and makes another six with the rest of the Magic team. Shaquille feels it's important for everyone to get a high school education.

And while Shaquille continues to give his time to help various people and organizations, there are many big corporations who want O'Neal to help sell their products. Shaq has done commercials for Pepsi and Reebok and produced a rap record. The record has been a huge hit. He has appeared on several late-night television talk shows, and has sold several thousand "Shaq Attack" T-shirts. Wherever you go in a mall or shopping center, Shaquille O'Neal's name and face can be seen in many storefronts.

Despite this overwhelming publicity, Shaquille O'Neal has remained the same. He has not forgotten who loved and cared about him before he became famous and rich. He is still humble and thankful for the good fortune he has had. With all the money, cars, success, fame, movies, and commercials, he is the same Shaquille O'Neal who grew up in Newark, New Jersey. "When [my dad] has a problem now, with either of my younger sisters, LaTeefah or Ayesha, or my brother, Jamal, he gets me on the phone and I have to talk to them," Shaq says. "I always tell my dad that he is getting soft. Thank God he wasn't soft when *I* was growing up."

Chapter 6

Sometimes respect is shown in a cruel fashion. At the 1994 All-Star Game in Minneapolis, O'Neal was always surrounded by three or four players whenever he got the ball. O'Neal had received 603,346 votes to outdistance Patrick Ewing once again for the starting center position. Yet he could barely get a shot off. It was the ultimate sign of respect for Shaquille. But it was disappointing for him and the fans who had come to see him perform his magic.

"It looked like people were jumping out of the first row of the stands to get him," said West center David Robinson of the San Antonio Spurs. "We wanted to block everything in the beginning of the game. We were going after *everything*."

Shaquille was the big name at the All-Star Game. When he received the ball down low for an opportunity to score, sometimes the entire West team defended against him. "They respect me," Shaq said. "Stuff isn't personal in this league. You guys [the media] are making it personal. I would have triple-teamed me down there, too. I wasn't frustrated. I was disappointed."

But O'Neal didn't have too much time to be disappointed. The Magic had played well in the first half of the 1993–94 season. Play-offs were a great possibility for Orlando, and Shaq didn't want to let that opportunity slip away.

Orlando's first opponents after the All-Star break were the Boston Celtics. Shaq and the Magic played well in the first three quarters but still trailed in the middle of the fourth, 84–79. Shaquille had already scored 23 points and pulled down 20 rebounds. The Magic needed some outside scoring to help Shaq out. Dennis Scott tried a long jumper from the left side but missed. Shaq, with his long right arm, snared the ball in one motion and slammed it through the basket. The Magic crowd roared after the jam.

The Magic got the ball down low to Shaq on their next possession. O'Neal faked and went up for a short hook. He missed but was fouled. It was Celtics center Robert Parish's sixth foul! He was out of the game! Now the Magic had another advantage with the Celtics' seven-footer not able to play anymore. O'Neal, not known for his foul shooting accuracy, made one of two free throws to cut the Celtics' lead to 84–82 with 5:25 left in the game.

Boston came right back on their possession when Dino Radja hit a jump shot, pushing the Celtics' advantage back to 86–82. Finally, Shaq got some help from his teammates. Donald Royal hit a driving layup. Then Anthony Bowie converted two foul shots to push the Magic into a tie at 86–86 with 4:19 left.

It was time for Shaquille to take over. Boston's Xavier McDaniel missed a jumper and the ball turned over to the Magic. With Parish out of the game, Orlando got the ball down by the left baseline to Shaq. He faked going to his left and spun back toward the baseline. Then he leaned in with a

San Antonio Spurs' center David Robinson guards Shaq. Like Robinson, Shaq is one of the most respected centers in the NBA.

short jumper that hit the glass and went in! Orlando had the lead, 88–86 with 3:10 to go.

But Boston was a tough team to beat any night. Their talented guard Dee Brown immediately ran down the floor and took a jumper from the right side. It went in to tie the score. Scott came right back to take another jumper for the Magic. It missed the mark. But Shaq stayed with the ball and was able to tip it into the basket over the Celtics' Ed Pickney. Now Orlando had the lead, 90–88 with 2:58 remaining.

Boston's Sherman Douglas hit two free throws to tie the game again. But Shaq was in no mood to let this game slip away at home. He got a pass down low. He faked and went up. It was blocked by Pickney. But the ball came right back to Shaq. O'Neal drove again and scored to give the Magic a 92–90 lead with 2:31 left.

The Celtics turned the ball over on their next possession. This was an opportunity for Orlando to put away their pesky opponents. The Magic relied on their main man again. Shaquille caught a pass along the right baseline, about 12 feet from the basket. Pickney had expected Shaq to drive on him but to his surprise O'Neal turned quickly. He launched a jumper as the Celtics' big man tried to block it. Too late! The ball floated over Pickney's right hand. Swish! The fans at Orlando were on their feet cheering for Shaquille. The Magic led, 94–90.

After Douglas missed a jump shot, Shaq came down with the rebound and got the ball to Anfernee Hardaway. Hardaway threw the ball down low to Shaq, who was surrounded by three Celtics. Instead of taking the shot over three people, O'Neal made a smart move. He threw a pass back to Hardaway, who was standing alone beyond the 3-point line. Hardaway took the shot. Swish! A 3-pointer!

Shaq gave the Orlando fans a special treat at the buzzer.

He had the ball alone and did a reverse slam, delighting the Magic fans. O'Neal finished with 36 points, 25 rebounds and 4 blocked shots. More importantly, the win moved the Magic one step closer to making the play-offs for the first time in their franchise history.

The Magic finished in second place behind the New York Knicks. It was a dream come true for the fans in Orlando. Before Shaquille O'Neal came along, they didn't expect much. Now, in Shaq's second year, the Magic found themselves in the NBA play-offs!

Orlando's first opponents were the Indiana Pacers. Their coach, Larry Brown, was one of the best. Indiana's strategy was simple. They would surround Shaquille and let the other Magic players try to hit the shots. It didn't work in the first half of Game 1. Shaquille was able to loosen up the Pacers' interior defense with several spinning moves and spectacular dunks. After one quarter the Magic led, 26–20.

Shaquille showed the same offensive skills in the second quarter. He was causing all sorts of problems for the Indiana forwards. Orlando led, 54–42, at halftime. It looked as if the Magic would get their first franchise play-off victory. But Brown was a master coach. He realized that one half of basketball did not mean that the game was over. Brown told his Indiana team to continue to triple-team Shaquille. The strategy started to work in the third quarter.

The Pacers, led by Reggie Miller and Rick Smits, cut the Orlando lead, 74–66, in the third quarter. Still, an 8-point lead wasn't bad. But the constant defensive pressure on O'Neal began to take its toll. Shaquille was having a hard time getting open underneath the basket. Several times in the fourth quarter, two and three Indiana Pacers would surround O'Neal. It forced him to be patient and try to find an open teammate somewhere to pass to. When he *did* find a teammate, sometimes the results were not good.

Indiana slowly climbed back into the game late in the fourth quarter. Shaquille had worked as hard as he could. He played the most minutes of anybody on either team. Exhausted and dripping from sweat from the wear and tear of playing against two and three Pacers at a time, Shaq walked onto the floor for the final ten seconds of Game 1.

Shaquille's 24-point effort and 19-rebound performance had helped Orlando hold their 88–86 lead. Indiana had the ball. Even if the Pacers scored, Shaq and his teammates believed they would still have a chance to win the game in overtime. But then Indiana did something amazing. Instead of trying to tie the game with the easier 2-point shot, the Pacers' Byron Scott surprised everybody. He shot a 3-pointer. And it was good!

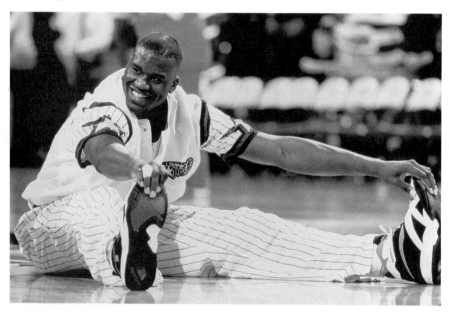

Shaq stretches before a game. Taking the Magic to its first ever trip to the play-offs, Shaq has become very popular with Orlando fans.

The Magic players were shocked. Nobody thought Scott would dare to take a long-range shot. But it was a risk that paid off for Indiana in this game, the first of the best-of-five. It was a short series and it was dangerous for the Magic to lose the first game at home.

Orlando never got back on track after losing Game 1. In Game 2, Shaquille O'Neal rarely was able to take a shot. He was hounded, surrounded, and harassed every time he touched the ball. Still, Shaq remained patient. He moved the ball outside in an effort to find open teammates. Few of them could connect on the jumpers except for Hardaway, who kept the Magic in the game until the final seconds with his scoring. Shaquille, who was also in foul trouble, scored a season-low 15 points, having faced triple-teaming most of the time. Orlando lost the second game, 103–101, and were one game away from the end of the season.

The Magic would *have* to win the next three games to move on to the second round. Even tougher, Orlando would have to win the next two games on the Pacers' home court. The Pacers used the same strategy in Game 3. They pushed and shoved Shaquille down underneath the basket to tire him out. At times, they put three men on him. Even so, Shaq was able to score 14 points in the first half. Orlando scored the last 10 points of the second quarter and led, 52–46.

But the Pacers were smart. They knew that Orlando would have to score without Shaquille if they triple-teamed the big guy. After three quarters, Indiana had pulled to within 72–68. There were still twelve minutes to play. The pressure on the other Magic players started to show. Their shots were not going in when Shaq got the ball to them.

The Magic were in deep trouble. Shaquille picked up his fifth foul with 9:22 left. He had to sit down on the bench. If he fouled once more he would be out of the game. Orlando was

With his monster slams and reverse dunks, Shaquille O'Neal continues to strive for the NBA championship.

still leading, 78–70. But Indiana scored the next 14 points as O'Neal watched helplessly from the bench.

It was too late when Shaquille re-entered the game. O'Neal scored the Magic's last basket of the season but that was with 4:18 left. Several Magic players missed 3-pointers in an attempt to get back into the game. Indiana's triple-team strategy had worked. Shaq scored a team-high 23 points. But he wasn't interested in statistics after that game.

Orlando was eliminated, 99–86, in three straight games. A season that had had so much promise ended in disappointment.

However, the Magic's future looks bright. They have the best young center in Shaquille O'Neal. The Magic also feature some of the other top young players in the league such as Nick Anderson and Anfernee Hardaway. And Shaq won't rest until an NBA championship comes to Orlando.

Despite the disappointment, Shaq made his summer of 1994 a positive one. He went back to LSU to take some courses. He had promised his mother that he would eventually get his college degree. And Shaq never wanted to break a promise to his mom.

The following season turned out to be even more successful for the Magic. After ending the season with the best record in the Eastern Conference, they moved into the playoffs. In the quarterfinals the Magic met the Chicago Bulls, who had been revived by the return of Michael Jordan. In a contest of wills between the two most famous names in basketball, the series went to five games, before the Magic finally defeated the Bulls. Shaq, who had a less-than-sizzling 53.3 percent in free-throws during the regular season, came back from his slump and shot 71.4 percent from the foul line.

Bursting through the semifinals the Magic defeated the Indiana Pacers. At last, the Magic would be playing in the finals! They would have their shot at a World Championship. Their opponent would be the World Champion Houston Rockets. Once again, however, experience was the victor, and the Magic fell in four straight games. Though there was once again no championship, the fledgling Magic moved one step further ahead. In a remarkable six years, the team moved from the bottom of the league to the NBA Finals. In only three seasons, Shaq has established himself as one of the top centers in the NBA. He was the NBA's top scorer for 1994–95, and was considered a contender for the MVP.

Going into the 1995–96 season the Magic's future looked bright. They had the best young center in Shaquille O'Neal. The Magic also featured some of the other top young players in the league such as Nick Anderson and Anfernee Hardaway. It would be no surprise if the Magic again appeared in the playoffs. As millions of fans agreed, a world championship would be only a matter of time.

Career Statistics

COLLEGE

Year	Team	GP	FG%	REB	PTS	AVG
1989-90	Louisiana State	32	.573	385	445	13.9
1990-91	Louisiana State	28	.628	411	774	27.6
1991-92	Louisiana State	30	.615	421	722	24.1
Totals		90	.610	1,217	1,941	21.6

NBA

Year	Team	GP	FG%	REB	AST	STL	BLK	PTS	AVG
1992-93	Orlando	81	.562	1,122	152	60	286	1,893	23.4
1993-94	Orlando	81	.599	1,072	195	76	223	2,377	29.3
1994-95	Orlando	79	.583	901	214	73	192	2,315	29.3
Totals		241	.583	3,095	561	209	701	6,585	27.3

Where to Write Shaquille O'Neal

Mr. Shaquille O'Neal
c/o Orlando Magic
1 Magic Place
Orlando, FL 32801

Index

SEP 2 6 2005

FEB 2 2 2006   APR 04

MAR 0 2 2006

MAR 1 0 2006   APR 2 8

MAR 2

MAR 2 9   MAR 0 9 2023
                       MAR 0 6 2024

APR 0 7 20

APR 1 9 20

MAY 1 5 20

SEP 1 9 2006

OCT 0 3 20

OCT 1 1 20

OCT 19 20

MAY 0 1

DATE DUE

PRINTED IN U.S.A.